HOW ANANSI CAPTURED THE STORY OF THE RAIN

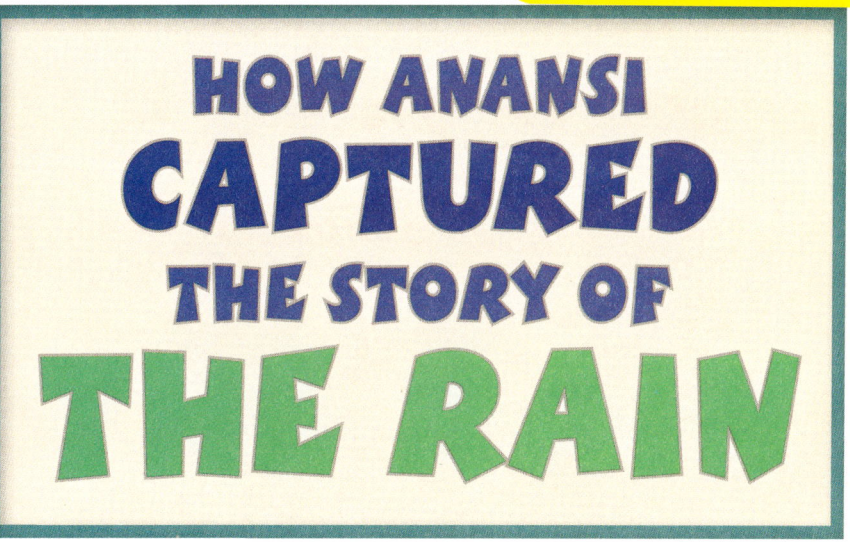

Retold by Claire Daniel
illustrated by Micha Archer

Scott Foresman
is an imprint of

PEARSON

Glenview, Illinois • Boston, Massachusetts • Chandler, Arizona •
Upper Saddle River, New Jersey

Illustrations
Micha Archer.

ISBN 13: 978-0-328-52675-8
ISBN 10:   0-328-52675-4

Copyright © by Pearson Education, Inc., or its affiliates. All rights reserved. Printed in the United States of America. This publication is protected by copyright, and permission should be obtained from the publisher prior to any prohibited reproduction, storage in a retrieval system, or transmission in any form or by any means, electronic, mechanical, photocopying, recording, or likewise. For information regarding permissions, write to Pearson Curriculum Rights & Permissions, One Lake Street, Upper Saddle River, New Jersey 07458.

Pearson® is a trademark, in the U.S. and/or in other countries, of Pearson plc or its affiliates.
Scott Foresman® is a trademark, in the U.S. and/or in other countries, of Pearson Education, Inc., or its affiliates.

2 3 4 5 6 7 8 9 10 V0N4 13 12 11 10

Long ago, in a time that no one can quite remember, the story of how to make rain fall from the sky was stolen and stored in a locked vault by Nyame, the sun. He did this because he had become upset when the rain and clouds blocked his shining rays. If he locked away this knowledge then his rays would always shine brightly from the sky.

At first, the animals on Earth enjoyed the abundance of sunshine. Plants thrived and fruits ripened; but after months and months of no rain, the plants began to wither and the roots of the trees thirsted for water. Grasses turned brown, streams stopped flowing, and lakes dried up to become cracked, parched expanses of mud.

All of the animal kingdom was desperate to learn how to make it rain, because without rain, all the plants would eventually die, and the food that the animals depended on would disappear.

Finally, the animals approached Anansi, a spider known for his trickery and cunning, to help them. If anyone could wrench this important story from Nyame, Anansi was the one to do it.

What the animals did not know about Anansi was that even though he projected himself as a master of trickery, it was actually his wife, Aso, who thought up the clever ideas—he only executed the ingenious plans she devised.

"I have a very bad feeling about this project," Anansi told Aso. "That sun is stubborn and untrustworthy, the worst sort you can deal with. Whatever am I going to do?"

"Dear Husband," she cooed. "Don't worry. I can help you outwit anyone. So have confidence. Find out what Nyame desires in return for his knowledge."

Although she kept it from her husband, Anansi's wife was growing tired of being in the shadows of her husband's feats. While he was lauded for his shrewdness and cleverness, she was forgotten and ignored. Aso made a plan to fool Anansi so that he would ultimately fail in his quest, and then she could run to his rescue. Everyone would see how brilliant and clever she was.

In the meantime, Anansi spun a golden strand of silk and climbed towards the sun to speak with Nyame.

Nyame was not happy to see Anansi. "What do you want?" Nyame asked menacingly, his hair lashing around him in angry blazes. Anansi smelled one of his leg hairs singe, but he did not back away.

"Your Excellency," he said, "with all respect due to the one who gives us light and warmth, I beseech you this day to give back the story of how to make rain fall from the sky."

Nyame's first reaction was to be annoyed by the spider's request.

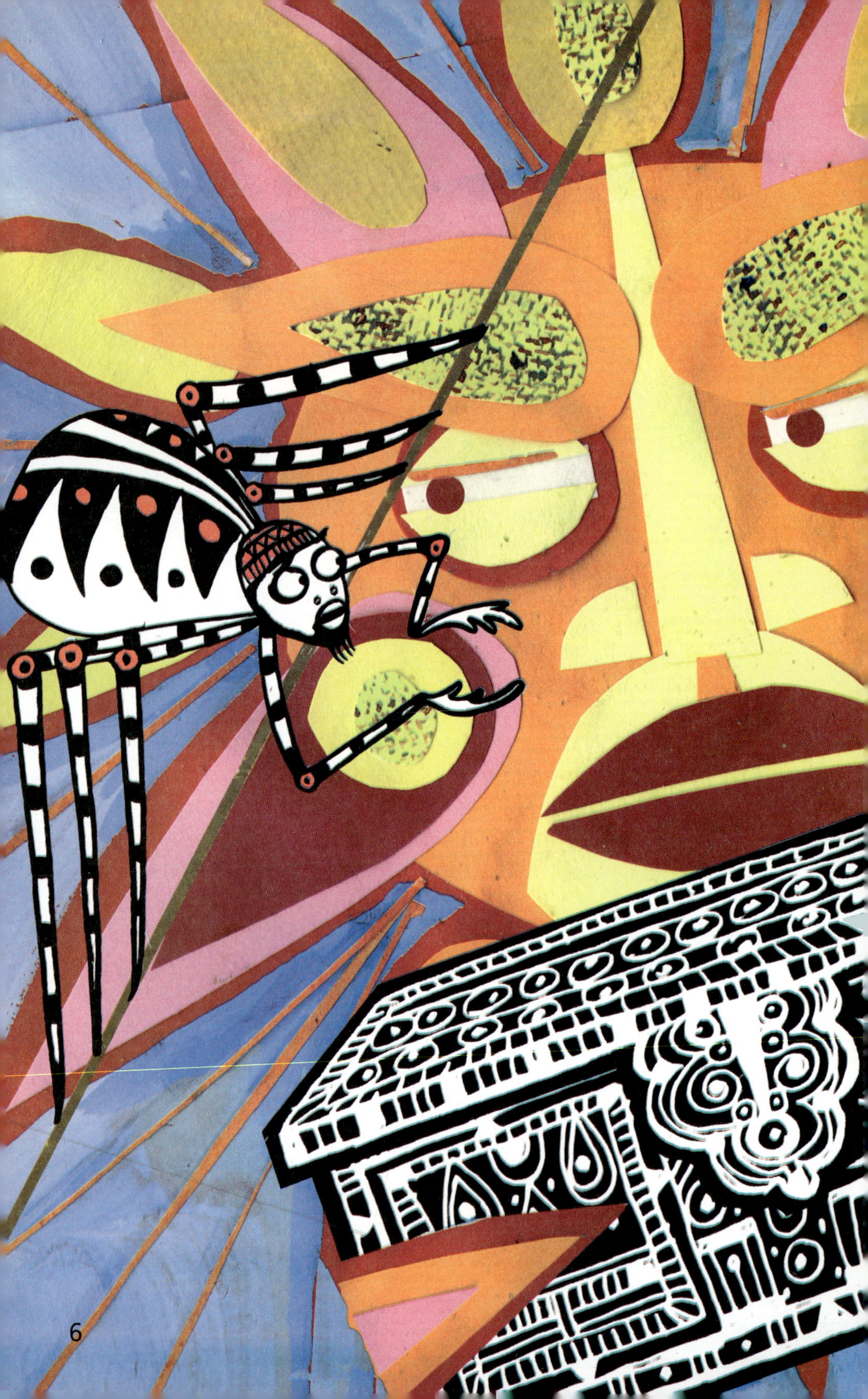

However, even Nyame had heard of Anansi's wit. He realized that Anansi might be able to entertain him. Of course, he had no intention of giving anything away, but it might be a pleasant diversion to see the creature fail.

Nyame replied, "Very well, I am prepared to give you the knowledge on one condition. You must complete three challenges for me. Then, and only then, can you have the knowledge."

Anansi thought of his clever wife's words. "Just tell me," he said, "and your tasks will be as good as done."

Nyame thought a moment and then said, "First, you must bring Mmoboro, the forty-seven hornets, to me. After that, you must deliver to me Onini, the great python. Last, you must bring me Osebo, the leopard. If you cannot complete all three tasks, then you and all the animal kingdom must forever leave me alone in peace!"

After hearing Nyame's requests, Anansi was not so confident. How could anyone capture Mmoboro, a fearsome collection of stinging hornets? How could he capture and deliver Onini, a huge python, who would certainly kill him before Anansi could move the snake an inch? And how could he capture Osebo, the leopard, one of the fastest-moving animals in the forest? Anansi wiped the sweat off his brow. He could feel his heart beating like a stampede of elephants.

Anansi went home and told his wife about the terrifying tasks he had been given to accomplish.

"These tasks are impossible," Anansi whimpered.

"Nonsense," Aso replied. She fed Anansi honey and yams to build his courage and poured him water to drink from a large dried gourd.

"Husband," she said, "you can accomplish these tasks easily if you do them one at a time. This hornet task, for instance—all you have to do is take this gourd with you, and when you get to the nest, shake the tree and tell the hornets to go inside the vessel."

Now Anansi's wife knew that the hornets would never succumb to such a suggestion, and in fact, they would probably sting Anansi in retaliation.

Aso planned to follow her husband with a strong, fine net. She would be there to capture the forty-seven hornets as they were punishing her husband for his stupidity.

After eating, Anansi began the trek to the tall tree where the Mmoboro made their home, but on the way, he became very thirsty. Seeing a stream next to the tree, he filled the gourd with water and poured it all over his body to cool himself. Then, as he climbed the tree, he continued drinking messily—so messily that he accidentally sprayed water inside the hornets' nest.

The forty-seven dripping wet hornets buzzed angrily inside the tree, since they were not accustomed to having rain fall inside their home. Anansi's wife looked on with glee at their anger and believed her plan was working far better than she had planned.

The angry, wet, and very confused hornets shot out of the tree to see what was happening. Before they could realize it wasn't raining, Anansi shouted, "Come and take shelter inside this gourd, and you will not get wet."

The forty-seven wet hornets quickly flew inside the hole of Anansi's gourd, and Anansi immediately plugged up the hole so the Mmoboro could not escape.

Aso was standing nearby and saw the entire incident, and she dropped the net in frustration. But she remembered that the saga was not over until all tasks had been completed, so she returned home to figure out how to advise her husband on the next challenge. Surely his latest accomplishment was only a fluke and not likely to be repeated.

Tucking the gourd under one of his eight arms, Anansi climbed the silk strand back up to Nyame and presented him with the gourd filled with the forty-seven hornets.

"Very good, clever spider," Nyame said disingenuously, with tight lips and a forced smile. "But I want to remind you that you still have two very difficult tasks to accomplish."

Anansi bowed to Nyame politely and took his leave, slipping down the rope. On the way down, he considered his incredible luck at capturing the Mmoboro. He fretted about how he could possibly capture Onini, the mighty python.

Once home, Anansi anxiously paced the floor, mumbling nervously to himself. Seeing his distress, Aso led him outside to a tall bamboo tree. She ordered him to cut it down.

Aso gave him a large sack and said, "When you see Onini, the python, tap him on the head three times with this bamboo pole, and he will fall to the ground. Then, you can tie him up in this sack."

"But Onini is big and strong!" Anansi protested. "If I tap him on the head, he will open his mouth and swallow me dead."

Now Aso knew this would be the outcome of such an action, but she figured she could cut open the snake and rescue her husband after she had captured him herself. And while he was recovering, she would take the snake to Nyame.

"Onini is a weak little snake," she said, "and is hardly as long as this pole. Have courage, dear husband!" She sounded very convincing.

Anansi carried the pole and the sack to the nearby river, where he knew Onini the python hunted for his prey. Following close behind was Aso, carrying a knife that she was sure she would need in order to rescue Anansi from the belly of Onini.

As he waited, Anansi began muttering, "I know she is wrong, and I am right. *I* say he is longer and stronger, and she says he is shorter and weaker. We should respect the mighty Onini in all his greatness!"

Onini was basking in the sun, and he jerked his head up at the mention of his name. Onini said, "Anansi, whatever on earth are you going on about? Are you talking to yourself?"

11

Anansi said, "I know, I must sound like a madman, but my wife is driving me crazy. It seems as if everything I say she questions or contradicts. For example, this very morning, we got into an argument about you."

Onini looked very pleased that he would spike controversy. "And what about me, dear fellow?" he asked.

Anansi replied, "My wife says that you are shorter and weaker than this pole. I, on the other hand, insist that you are longer and stronger."

"It must be distressing to have such a foolish wife. Why don't we measure to see whether I am indeed longer and stronger than this pole?" Onini suggested.

"Maybe you could just stretch your head as far as you can go to the far end of the pole," Anansi told Onini.

Onini stretched out, and Anansi pretended to measure him.

Then he said, "Very good, but your tail won't stay still. Do you mind if I tie it to the end of the pole to keep it in one place?"

Onini agreed, and Anansi used a nearby vine to tie Onini's tail to the pole. Onini looked back as Anansi seemingly inspected Onini's tail.

"Hmm . . . ," Anansi said with a furrowed brow.

"What is it?" Onini asked, worried that the pole might be longer than him.

"You look a little short. If you stretch a little more, I can hold you in place with the vine," Anansi suggested.

Onini stretched and stretched, and Anansi wound and wound the vine until it completely wrapped around the pole and the python's body. Onini couldn't move a muscle.

"Oh dear," Anansi said. "I suppose that my wife was correct, for you are shorter than this pole, and since you can't move away from it, you are also weaker."

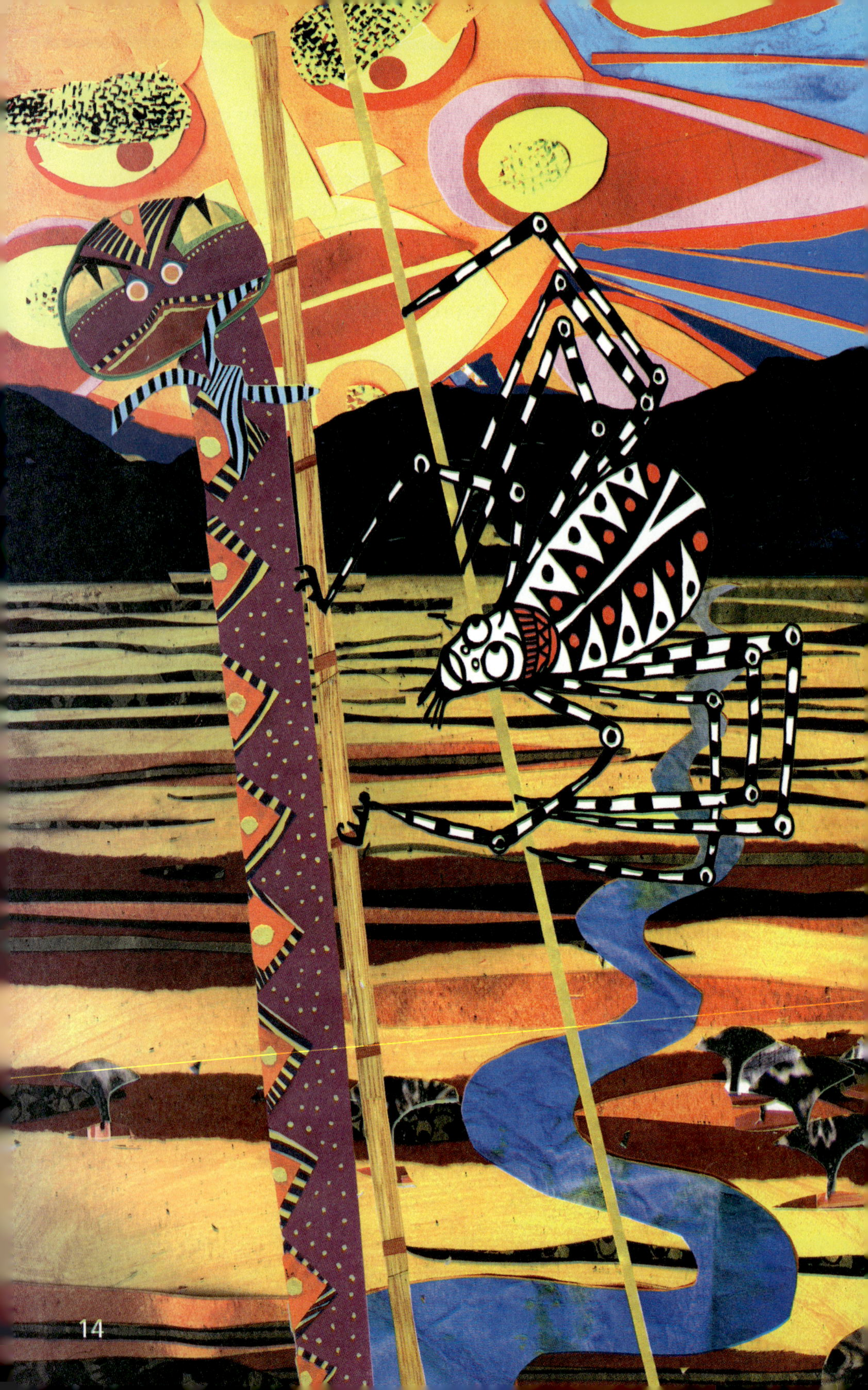

Anansi felt quite taken with himself because he hadn't needed to tap Onini with the pole and risk his life. But Aso, seeing that her husband had succeeded in trapping the python, stomped off in frustration. Back home, she said to herself, *My next plan must work or no one will ever know that I am cleverer than my husband.*

Anansi shouldered the pole with Onini tied to it and skittered up the silk rope to Nyame, who was less than pleased to see Anansi accompanied by the python.

Still, the Sun was not too worried about Anansi's success. Capturing Osebo, the leopard, would be an impossible undertaking, even for this ambitious spider.

Anansi slid back down the rope to his house and asked his wife to fill him in on a plan for his next task. He was proud of his success, but knew that that luck had enabled him to capture the python and the forty-seven hornets. He was extremely anxious about his chances of capturing Osebo, the leopard.

His wife told him, "Husband, there is no need to be nervous. All you need to do is invite Osebo to play a game with you. Tell him that, just for fun, you'll take turns tying each other up with this vine. Tell him you want to go first, but then allow him to go first. When he is bound, you can deliver him to Nyame."

"Do you think that could work?" Anansi asked. He was concerned that Osebo was too smart to fall for this scheme.

"Of course!" she said. "Remember, leopards aren't clever like spiders."

His wife's confidence in the plan was all Anansi needed; he knew that Aso was one of the cleverest spiders anywhere. Happy with the plan, Anansi felt he could accomplish this last task.

But there was something Aso failed to tell him: she had dug a pit near Osebo's house and covered the hole with palm leaves. She knew Osebo was not naïve enough to fall for the game Anansi would propose, and she would come to his rescue by trapping the fast-moving leopard in the hole.

The next day, Anansi arrived at Osebo's house, but before he could propose any kind of game, he fell into Aso's pit! Since Anansi was a spider, he had no trouble climbing out of the pit. However, just as he was about to scamper out, Osebo happened to amble by and see Anansi. Now, Osebo was a mighty leopard, and he was mightily hungry. Anansi looked like a tasty snack to him. Osebo thought it was his turn to trick the trickster spider.

"Anansi, my friend!" he said. "It's so nice to see you. Why don't you climb out of there? We can have breakfast together!" Osebo licked his lips in anticipation of his spidery meal.

Anansi was much too clever to fall for the leopard's trick, so he replied, "Oh, but breakfast would be much tastier if you came down into the pit with me." Without thinking it through, Osebo let his stomach do his thinking. He jumped into the pit after Anansi. As soon as he landed on the bottom, he realized that he had no way of getting out.

And that's when Anansi realized he could use his wife's plan after all to trick the leopard.

"I'm so foolish," Anansi said. "I didn't realize that you could not climb out as easily as I. Why don't you let me climb out first, and then I will lower a ladder for you? Then we can enjoy a delicious breakfast together."

Behind a nearby bush, Aso was watching nervously. She hoped her husband was okay; she wanted him to fail, but she did not want him to be eaten! She then saw Anansi climbing out of the pit and her heart lifted.

Osebo, seeing no other way out of his predicament, allowed the spider to climb out of the pit. Once he reached the top, Anansi tied a sturdy vine to the top of a sapling.

He then bent the sapling toward the ground and tied the other end of the vine to a nearby rock. He took another vine and threw it to Osebo in the pit. He told the leopard to catch the vine and tie it securely to his tail.

"The vine is tied tightly around my tail," Osebo yelled up to Anansi.

"Very well," said Anansi. "Now throw me the other end of the vine."

Anansi tied the other end of Osebo's vine to the top of the sapling, and cut the other vine that held the sapling to the rock. The sapling straightened, and Osebo came flying out of the pit and dangled by his tail from the sapling. The leopard screamed and struggled to get free, causing him to swing around and around and around.

Anansi waited until Osebo became dizzy, and then tied his front and back legs with the vine as well. Anansi cut down the sapling and carried Osebo to the silk rope.

Having witnessed the entire event, Anansi's wife, Aso, was pleasantly surprised at her husband's ingenuity. He had carried out the exact plan she had intended to use to catch the mighty leopard, Osebo. Pride replaced jealousy and resentment, and she accompanied her husband to present Nyame with the final success. She also intended to make sure that Nyame made good on his promise and delivered the story of how to make it rain.

When Nyame saw Anansi and Aso scampering up the silken rope with Osebo tied to the vine, he began to despair, as he knew that he had been outsmarted.

As he presented Osebo the leopard, Anansi stood next to his wife. "Nyame, your Excellency," he said proudly, "we have completed the last and final task."

Nyame was disappointed at having to give up his treasure, but was impressed with Anansi's success. "Very well, Anansi, you have earned the knowledge of how to make rain fall from the sky."

Nyame continued with his praise. "You are a very clever spider . . ."

Anansi interrupted Nyame with surprising words. "Oh no, great Sun, none of this was my doing. All credit should go to my clever wife, Aso. It was her plan that enabled me to capture Mmoboro, the forty-seven hornets. She came up with the scheme that captured Onini, the mighty python. And Osebo, the fast-moving leopard, owes his captivity to her. I was merely the executor of *her* clever plans."

Nyame turned to Aso, who was standing taller than before. He admired her ability to outsmart him, and as he handed over the chest containing the knowledge of how to make it rain, he shone a beam of light onto Aso so that all of the animal kingdom could look up in the sky and see that Nyame had honored her. Aso beamed in pleasure at the public acknowledgment of her wit.

Aso graciously said to Nyame, "Thank you, Nyame, for returning this important knowledge to the animal kingdom, but don't grieve its loss. The animal kingdom will still bask in your shining rays. We need your light and warmth as much as we need the rain."

Nyame smiled in response to Aso's compassionate words and shone brightly. They say to this day that when skies become cloudy and gray and it begins to rain, Nyame no longer gets upset. And when the clouds and the rains clear, he shines even brighter.

The Water Cycle

In this tale, the animal kingdom needed the knowledge of how to make it rain. In truth, rain occurs on its own as a product of the water cycle.

As the Sun shines down on Earth's oceans, lakes, rivers, streams, and even puddles, water evaporates and releases into the air as water vapor. This water vapor travels high into the atmosphere. As the air turns colder, the water vapor condenses, forming tiny droplets of water.

These water droplets form clouds. When clouds become too dense, precipitation falls to Earth in the form of rain, snow, sleet, or hail. The precipitation refills Earth's oceans, lakes, rivers, streams, and puddles and seeps into the soil to help the plants grow. Then, the water cycle begins again!